Tell me about...

Baseball

Published in 2009 by Evans Publishing Ltd,
2A Portman Mansions,
Chiltern St, London WIU 6NR

Editor: Nicola Edwards
Designer: D.R. Ink
All photographs by Wishlist except for p6 Jeff Zelevansky/Stringer/Getty Images; p7 Rich
Pilling/Stringer/MLB Photos via Getty Images; p9 Jim Rogash/Stringer/Getty Images; p10 Paul
Spinelli/Contributor/MLB Photos via Getty Images; p11 Jamie Squire/Getty Images;
p12 Andy Hayt/Getty Images; p16 matooker/iStock; p22 Doug Pensinger/Getty Images;
p23 John Iacono /Sports Illustrated/Getty Images; p25 FREDERIC J. BROWN/AFP/Getty Images; p26
OMAR TORRES/AFP/Getty Images; p27 Rich Pilling/MLB via Getty Images

British Library Cataloguing in Publication Data

Gifford, Clive
  Baseball. -- (Tell me about sport)
  1. Baseball -- Juvenile literature.
  I. Title II. Series
  796.3'57-dc22

ISBN-13: 9780237538347

Printed in China.

The author and publisher would like to thank Colette Keating, James Knowles, Perrie Sherman, Courtney
Singleton, C.J Singleton, Fiona Sheppard and Coach Keith Sherman for their participation in the making
of this book. Thanks also to Baseball MK Club and Walton High School.

Contents

Baseball

Jason Bartlett (in grey) of the Tampa Bay Rays dives to reach home plate. He is tagged out though by Philadelphia's Carlos Ruiz. Baseball features many moments of great excitement like this.

Baseball is an exciting sport of skill and strategy. Two teams, each containing nine players, have nine innings in which to bat and try to score runs. A run is scored when a player reaches and touches each of the bases on the baseball field (first, second and third base) and then reaches home plate.

When not batting, a team is in the field. They try to get the other team's players out and stop them scoring runs. The team with the most runs at the end of the nine innings wins. There are no ties or draws in baseball so if the scores are level, further innings are played until a team has won.

A batting team's innings lasts until three of its players are out. Players are out if they hit the ball and it is caught by a fielder before it touches the ground. A player who hits three

Interesting innings

In 1981, a minor league game between the Pawtucket Red Sox and the Rochester Red Wings lasted an astonishing 33 innings before Pawtucket finally won 3-2.

The biggest thrashing in recent times in Major League Baseball was in 2007. The Texas Rangers beat the Baltimore Orioles 30-3.

▲ The pitcher is the player who throws the ball towards the batter. On a baseball field, he or she throws from a raised mound 18 metres away from the batter. The pitcher's team-mate, the catcher, is behind the batter.

strikes (see p17) is also out. The fielding side can also tag out a runner by touching him or her with the ball when the runner isn't standing on a base.

At the highest levels, in professional leagues such as Major League Baseball (MLB) in the United States and Canada, baseball is watched by tens of thousands of fans in stadiums and millions more on television. One of the great things about the sport, though, is that a few friends can enjoy catching and pitching with just a bat and ball in a park or in another wide open space.

◄

One or more umpires run a game of baseball. In the highest levels of the sport such as Major League Baseball (MLB), a team of umpires is headed by the umpire in chief or home plate umpire who stands behind the batter and catcher.

Hitting home runs

At the centre of a game of baseball is the fascinating duel between the batter and the pitcher. The batter wants to hit the ball into play but most of all wants to hit a home run. This happens when the batter hits the ball far enough to be able to run around all the bases and get back to home plate in one go.

Most home runs are scored by batters hitting the ball over the outfield fence so that they can jog round the bases and celebrate at home plate. A small number of home runs are scored even though the ball remains in

▶
This player aims to hit the ball powerfully. If the ball bounces and then goes over the fence, it is not a home run but the hitter goes to second base.

Home runs

Babe Ruth hit 40 or more home runs in a season not once or twice but for an incredible 11 seasons. He managed 2,217 runs batted in (see p9) during his career.

In 1997, the Seattle Mariners team hit a record 264 home runs in the season. The Texas Rangers almost matched them in 2005, hitting 260.

In Japan, Sadaharu Oh hit 868 home runs during 22 seasons playing for the Yomiuri Giants.

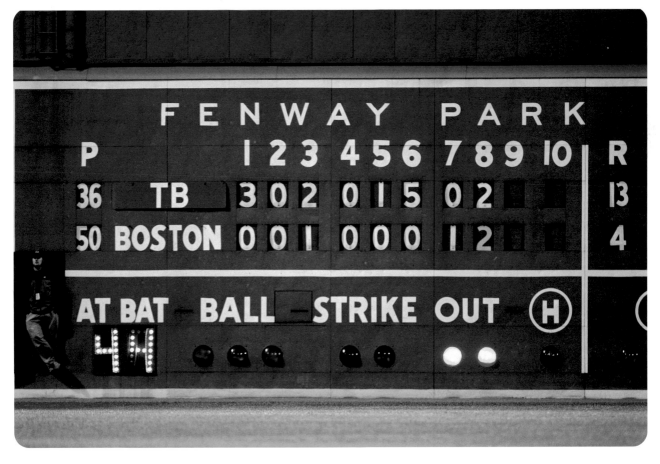

▲ This scoreboard shows that the Tampa Bay Rays (TB) lead the Boston Red Sox by 13 runs to 4 (far right) in the eighth inning. The home team always bats bottom (second) in an inning.

the park. They occur when the ball is hit away from the fielders or because of fielding errors.

Once a batter has hit the ball and heads to first base, he or she becomes a runner. Team-mates who have already batted and become runners may be on other bases. A batter's hit might result in one of these other runners reaching home plate and scoring a run. Any runs scored as a result of a batter's hit are credited to his or her statistics as a run batted in (RBI).

When a batter has team-mates on first, second and third bases, it is said that the bases are loaded. Batters who can hit a home run in this situation will gain their team a grand slam as they and the other three players each score a run.

The baseball field

Baseball is played on a large field. The left and right edges of the field are marked by foul lines which meet at the home plate and then fan outwards. A ball hit over a foul line is out of play and won't count as a hit. The batter has to be careful because the fielders can still catch a high ball in foul territory. Foul poles are tall poles which officials use to judge whether a foul ball has been hit or not.

The infield is made up of the area containing the three bases and home plate which form a diamond shape. The

▼ This diagram shows the typical field markings and positions of a fielding team.

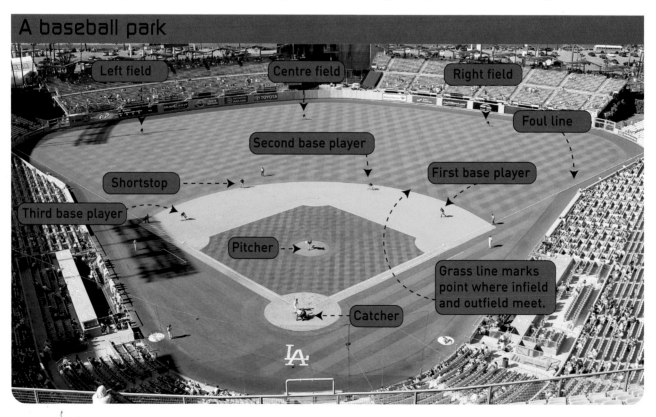

A baseball park

Left field

Centre field

Right field

Foul line

Second base player

First base player

Shortstop

Third base player

Pitcher

Grass line marks point where infield and outfield meet.

Catcher

distance between each base is 27.4m in Major League Baseball but smaller diamonds are often used for young players. Each base is a 38cm foam square whilst the home plate is 42cm across and made of rubber which is coloured white.

Infields and outfields

The tallest outfield wall in Major League Baseball is the 11.3m-high wall at Fenway Park, home of the Boston Red Sox. It is known as the Green Monster.

Minute Maid Park, the home of the Houston Astros, has a flagpole in the field of play! In 2003, the Milwaukee Brewers' Richie Sexson became the first person to hit the ball onto the flagpole.

The outfield runs from the infield to the outfield fence or wall. Outfields vary in size and the outfield wall in height. This means that it is easier to hit runs and home runs at some parks than others.

Outside the field of play, there are a number of other features at a typical baseball ground. These include team dugouts where players sit while waiting to play and the bullpen where pitchers practise before entering the game.

◀ This fielder wears a typical baseball uniform – a comfortable baseball jersey, a cap, baseball pants and special shoes with cleats which grip the ground. A large but well-fitting glove is used to help catch and field the ball.

▶ A batter has to stand in one of the two batting boxes on either side of home plate (depending on whether the batter is left- or right-handed). A batter wears a protective helmet and often wears a batting glove to strengthen his or her grip.

Star players

The major leagues are the peak of baseball and home to most of the world's finest players. Many are millionaires because the 30 MLB teams often pay large salaries to attract the players with the greatest skills. Top players such as Alex Rodriguez, Ryan Howard and Manny Ramirez are famous celebrities in the United States.

Despite their wealth and fame, players have to train and work hard. Spring training camp begins in February and lasts almost two months. Thousands of fans flock to exhibition matches played during this period.

▼

The Los Angeles Dodgers perform stretches before taking batting practice. In the middle is star player, Manny Ramirez wearing number 99. He has hit over 520 home runs.

▲ First baseman, Conor Jackson makes a diving stop at full stretch. See how in the background, his team-mate runs to cover him should he not stop the ball.

Players have to be at the peak of fitness for the start of the season in April. Ahead of them is a gruelling schedule. Each team plays a staggering 162 games in the season which runs until October. The winner of each of the MLB's six divisions plus the two best runners-up enter the play-offs. Then the top two teams play a best-of-seven-game World Series for the ultimate prize of best team of the season.

Baseball winners

The New York Yankees have won 26 World Series, 16 more than the second-placed team, the St Louis Cardinals.

Injuries and loss of form affect most players at some point. This is why Cal Ripken's record is so remarkable. He began a run of continuous games for the Baltimore Orioles in 1982 and kept on playing without missing a game until 1998, an amazing total of 2,632 games.

Alex Rodriguez is one of baseball's finest ever batters with over 550 MLB home runs. In 2007, he signed a contract with the New York Yankees worth over US$270 million over eight years!

Fielding

At the highest level, crowds at MLB games thrill to see spectacular diving stops or acrobatic high leaps. All fielding, though, is crucial to the pitching team as the players try to stop any runs being scored.

All players, including the pitcher, must be skilled fielders. This only comes with hundreds of hours of practice. Players work hard to become really skilled at fielding ground balls zipping across the grass and at catching balls in the air travelling at different heights and angles. Players learn to follow the ball's path on the ground or in the air and to throw fast, accurate returns.

Fielders wear a glove on their weaker hand, allowing them to throw with their stronger hand and arm. This takes

▶
This fielder is in the ready position. His legs are spread with his knees bent and his head forward watching the ball and ready to move quickly to field it.

▼ This outfielder has got into a good position to catch a fly ball – a ball high in the air. Her eyes watch the ball right into her glove.

▲ Crouching low to field a ground ball, this outfielder springs up quickly. As he does, he takes the ball from his glove, turns and steps forward as he releases a powerful, accurate throw.

some time to get used to. Coaches work with young players to help them to get used to the glove and know how to keep the ball in it.

When a ball makes it beyond the infield, the three outfielders have to run down the ball and return it. Outfielders need powerful arms to make strong but accurate throws. When the ball is fielded deep (a long way away from home plate), one of the infielders will move and act as a cut-off. This is a player who catches the outfielder's throw and then throws it to a base player or the catcher.

Pitching

The pitcher is a vitally important player to the fielding team. Top pitchers can throw a ball over 150km/h but the very best also have great control of the ball's path.

Good pitchers are able to throw different types of pitch which travel in different ways to the batter. Some pitchers also release pitches from different arm angles, making it harder for the batter to work out the flight of the ball.

▼ This baseball pitcher starts his pitching movement by winding up. He then uncoils, steps forward and unleashes a powerful throw.

◀
Different grips are used to throw different types of pitch. The fastball (left) travels straight through the air at speed to the batter. The curveball (right) spins out of the hand and swerves through the air.

A good pitch must pass between the batter's knees and back shoulder in the normal batting stance and pass across part of the home plate. If the batter doesn't swing, or swings and misses a ball thrown in the strike zone, or swings at but misses a ball outside of the strike zone, it's a strike against the batter. Three strikes and the batter is out.

Pitchers must also field balls that are hit or bunted (see p21) towards them. They can stop an opposing runner stealing a base by throwing the ball sharply to a base player. If a pitcher starts a pitching movement and then turns and throws the ball to a baseman to get the runner out, the umpire will signal a balk. When this happens, the runner and the hitter all advance one base.

▼ This imaginary box is called the strike zone. Pitches which travel inside this box and are not hit are strikes; those outside it are known as balls. If four balls are pitched at a batter, the batter walks to first base.

The catcher

The catcher stands close behind the batter and home plate and must field the ball if it is pitched and gets past the batter. A catcher must have a good knowledge of the batters so that he or she can suggest what sort of ball the pitcher should throw next. Catchers let the pitcher know with hand and finger signals, so the batter doesn't know what type of pitch is coming next.

As some pitches reach the catcher at speeds of over 150km/h, plenty of protective clothing is really important. Catchers wear an athletic supporter to protect the groin area, a helmet with a faceguard and throat protector, a chest protector and leg and

▼ This catcher is in a good, balanced stance, crouched but light on his feet so that he can spring in any direction. His head is level with his eyes on the play.

▼ This catcher is signalling two fingers down to the pitcher. This may mean that the pitcher should throw a curve ball.

ankle guards. They catch and field the ball with a padded mitt, larger than a regular fielder's glove.

Catchers have a tough job. They have to be alert and agile to catch a pitch cleanly that might curve down or away from them at the last second. A catcher must also be ready to leap up to catch a high ball and to throw accurately to a base to throw out a base runner.

If the ball is hit, the catcher's job isn't necessarily over. Catchers may have to block home plate and be ready to catch the ball to tag out a runner who is trying to score a run.

▲ A ball that hits the edge of the bat can often 'pop up' high into the air. The catcher hops up, lifts off his mask to give himself a clear view of the ball's position and moves quickly under the ball to catch it.

◄ This catcher throws the ball quickly and accurately to his first baseman. A good throw can run a runner out.

Batting

Players bat in an order decided by the coach. Teams give a lot of thought to their batting order to make sure that their best hitters are placed in key positions.

A batter stands in one of the two batting boxes depending on whether they are right- or left-handed. Batters need a good eye, quick reflexes and great timing to judge whether a pitch will be inside their strike zone and, if they decide to go for it, to connect well with the ball using a powerful swing.

If a batter swings and misses the ball, he or she will receive a strike. A batter also gains a first or second strike if he or she hits a foul ball. If the batter hits a foul ball whilst already on two strikes, he or she receives a further pitch.

▼ The batter begins with his bat drawn back and his weight on his back foot. He steps towards the pitcher with his front foot and turns his hips and then his shoulders to pull the bat through. He aims for his bat to meet the ball powerfully with a snap of his wrists and then a long follow-through.

▲ This player is bunting the ball. She has turned to face the pitcher, slid her right hand up the bat and presented it to the ball to give it a gentle tap.

▲ A batter grips the bat. The hands are close together and the grip is not too tight.

Sometimes, instead of a long swing, batters try a different technique called bunting. A bunt is a gentle hit used to surprise the fielding team either to get the batter to first base or to sacrifice himself by getting out so that a runner from his team advances a base.

There are other ways the batter can get to first base besides making a good hit or receiving four balls. One is if the batter is hit by a pitch outside of the strike zone and did not swing. Another is called 'catcher interference'. This happens when batters are swinging inside the batting box, and their bat touches any part of the catcher.

Infielders

Apart from the pitcher and catcher, there are four infielders – first, second and third base players and the shortstop. The shortstop has the busiest fielding position of all. Shortstops must be very alert and quick across the ground to catch or field the ball. What they do next can be crucial as they may also be able to throw to a base player or tag an opponent out.

Tagging out an opponent occurs when a runner who is not touching base is touched with the ball in a fielder's hand. When runners slide in towards a base, base players may hold the ball in their glove in front of their base so that the runner touches their glove before the base and is out.

▼ Darwin Barney fields a throw as runner Mike Cavasinni dives spectacularly to try to steal second base. Infielders need quick reactions to catch, throw and tag out runners.

In some situations, the runner does not have to be touched to be out. When a runner is forced to run, a base player can touch the base while holding the ball and the runner heading towards that base is forced out.

Good, sharp fielding can sometimes lead to a double play, where two opponents are both out on the same play. For instance, a catch may be made and then a throw made to a base player to put out another player. A triple play is three batters or runners all out on the same play.

Plays

Cleveland's Asdrubal Cabrera managed to make a triple play all by himself against the Toronto Blue Jays in 2008. He dived and caught the ball, stepped onto a base to remove a second player and then tagged out a third player. It was the 14th ever unassisted triple play in Major League Baseball history.

In 2005, St Louis Cardinals' first baseman, Albert Pujols made 175 double plays in the season. This was the most by an MLB player in 39 years.

▼ Jason Bartlett of the Tampa Bay Rays dives for home plate but is tagged out by the Philadelphia Phillies catcher, Carlos Ruiz.

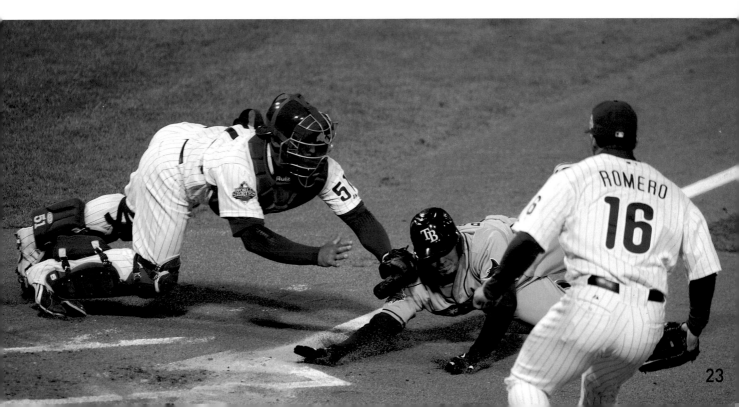

Running and stealing

As soon as a player hits the ball into play, he or she must start running as fast as possible to safely reach first base. Runners aim to touch the nearest part of it with their foot before they can be tagged or before the ball reaches the first base player who can put a runner out.

Runners are allowed to run past first base providing they touch it on the way. A runner cannot overrun second or third base. This is one of the reasons why many players, at the end of their run to the base, slide in order to reach the base. Once runners have reached base, if they still touch it, they cannot be tagged out. When runners try to run two or more bases in a row, they tend to run in a curve, leaning away from the base and touching the inside of it as they sprint hard towards the next base.

▼ This runner slides along the ground to successfully make second base. His front foot is kept just up off the ground and his hands are up to avoid injury.

Stealing a base happens when a runner manages to advance to the next base while the pitcher is pitching the ball. Stealing a base takes great cunning and timing as well as explosive sprinting speed. Runners have to watch the pitcher carefully. If they set off too early, the pitcher might turn and throw to the base so that the runner can be tagged out. This is known as a pickoff.

Successful steals

Rickey Henderson is the all-time leader in Major League Baseball for stolen bases with a huge total of 1,406.

In 2007, the Seattle Mariners' Ichiro Suzuki completed his 45th successful steal in a row – a record in Major League Baseball.

▼ Hiroyuki Nakajima from Japan's 2008 Olympic team sprints from first base as the pitcher makes his pitch. He hopes to steal second base.

The world of baseball

Baseball was developed in the United States and has been exported all around the world. The home of baseball has the strongest and most popular competition, Major League Baseball, with its two leagues, the National (NL) and American League (AL).

Below these two leagues are a large collection of minor leagues in the USA and Canada. These leagues also pay professionals to play. Many of their players hope that one day they will play in the Major League.

Outside of North America, baseball is played in over 100 countries. Japan was the first of many Asian countries including South Korea, Taiwan and China to have professional leagues.

▼ Cuba's Norberto Gonzalez pitches the ball during the final of the 2008 Olympics baseball competition. Cuba's opponents South Korea won 3-2.

▲ Eric Bruntlett slides into home plate to score the winning run in the third game of the 2008 World Series. Bruntlett's team, the Philadelphia Phillies won the series four games to one.

The sport was first played in Cuba in the 1870s and then spread to other Caribbean countries such as Puerto Rico and Dominican Republic as well as to Central and South America. More than 20 per cent of the players in Major League Baseball are from Caribbean or Latin American nations.

There are many competitions for national teams. In Europe, a championship is held every two years with the Netherlands winning and Great Britain coming second in the 2007 competition. The World Baseball Classic, set up by Major League Baseball, features 16 national teams from around the world. Japan won the first competition in 2006 beating South Korea in the single game final, 10-6.

Major competitions

In 2004 the Boston Red Sox swept the World Series in four games, beating the St. Louis Cardinals. It was exciting because the Red Sox had not won a championship in 86 years!

The first MLB game to be played outside of Canada or the United States occurred in 1996 in Monterrey, Mexico. Since then, MLB games have been played in Puerto Rico and Japan.

Where next?

These websites will help you to find out more about baseball.

http://www.mlb.com/mlb/kids/

This is the kids section of the massive Major League Baseball website with games, interviews with star players and lots of other news and views.

http://www.ducksters.com/sports/baseballpositions.php

This small collection of webpages offers a clear guide to basic baseball player positions, strategy and rules.

http://www.howbaseballworks.com/

A handy website with explanations of many parts of Major League Baseball from pitching and scoring to baseball statistics.

http://www.sikids.com/

The famous *Sports Illustrated* magazine has a special website for younger web surfers. It contains lots of fun games as well as news, results and a player search for all the teams in the MLB.

http://www.baseballsoftballuk.com/

BSUK is an organisation developing baseball and softball in the UK. Its website has details of baseball clubs and leagues searchable by region.

http://www.britishbaseball.org/

This is the home on the internet of the British Baseball Federation. It contains news, a calendar of games and events and details of clubs around the country.

Baseball words

bases the four points of the baseball diamond, labelled in order, first, second and third base and finally, home plate

bunting a batting technique in which you tap the ball gently to surprise the other team and score a run or reach a base

home plate the base which the batter stands over as he or she tries to hit the ball

home run when a batter makes a fair hit, usually over the fence, and touches each of the three bases and, finally, home plate in a row

infield the diamond-shaped part of the playing field which has the bases at its corners

inning the period of time it takes both teams to bat

outfield the part of the playing area outside of the infield

pitch a throw made by the pitcher from the pitching mound towards the batter

run a score made by a player who makes it round the bases and touches home plate without being out

shortstop a fielding position between second and third base

tagout a runner is tagged out if he or she has not touched a base and has been touched by a fielder holding the ball

umpires officials who run a game of baseball

Index